First published in 2007 by
Carlton Books Limited
20 Mortimer Street
London W1T 3JW

Text and design copyright © 2007 Carlton Books Limited

Arsenal.com

A CIP catalogue record of this book is available from the British Library

ISBN: 978–1–84442–852–6

Commissioning Editor: Martin Corteel
Project Art Director: Darren Jordan
Design: Ben Ruocco
Picture Reserarch: Paul Langan
Editorial Assistant: David Ballheimer
Production: Peter Hinton

Printed in Italy

The publishers would like to thank the following sources for their kind
permission to reproduce the pictures in this book.

Courtesy of Cadbury Schweppes PLC: 57b-2

iStockphoto: 49l, 57t-1, 57t-2, 57t-3, 57t-4, 57t-5, 57c-1, 57c-4,
57c-5, 57b-1.

PA Photos: 32, 34; /Jon Buckle/Empics Sport: 39tr; /David
Cheskin: 49br; /Barry Coombs/Empics Sport: 38bl, 39b; /Mike
Egerton/Empics Sport: 45tr; /Empics Sport: 45tl; /Matthew Fearn:
57c-2; /Nigel French/Empics Sport: 39r; /Hahn-Liewig/ABACA: 43;
/Petr David Josek/AP: 38tr; /Tony Marshall/Empics Sport: 38br,
44tl; /Martin Meissner/AP: 38tl; /Andrew Milligan: 48br; /NASA
Planetary Photojournal: 57c-3; /Ian Nicholson: 48t; /Eraldo Peres/
AP: 49tr; /S&G: 33; /Jorge Saenz/AP: 44tr; /Sang Tan/AP: 39tl,
57b-4; /John Walton/Empics Sport: 39bl, 39br.

Rex Features: /Everett Collection: 57b-3

Every effort has been made to acknowledge correctly
and contact the source and/or copyright holder of each
picture and Carlton Books Limited apologises for
any unintentional errors or omissions which will be
corrected in future editions of this book.

All other images kindly supplied by
Arsenal Football Club: Photographers
Stuart MacFarlane and David Price

The Official
Arsenal
Annual 2008

Chas Newkey-Burden

CARLTON
BOOKS

CONTENTS

Dear Supporters,

Welcome to the Official Arsenal Annual 2008.

It was an eventful and exciting first season at Emirates Stadium, with a number of positives to take us into a new campaign. A group of truly exciting young players has emerged to first-team reckoning thanks to their tremendous run in the Carling Cup, and once again we have given ourselves the chance to play a part in European football via the Champions League qualifiers. I hope you will agree that, across all competitions, some of the football the team has played has been simply breathtaking.

Our league record against Manchester United, Chelsea and Liverpool – our fellow top four teams – was fantastic, and we know that with a little more consistency in 2007–08 we can mount a strong challenge for the Premiership title. We are equally confident that we can once more reach the UEFA Champions League Final this coming season.

With a new stadium and such a gifted young squad there is no shortage of confidence and optimism at the club. As expected it took a short while to settle in at our new home but the victories over Liverpool, Manchester United and Tottenham certainly demonstrated that we all now feel at home there.

In closing, may I take this opportunity to thank you, the Arsenal supporters, for your loyal and vocal support during the 2006–07 campaign. You are a key part of every victory we enjoy and I know I speak for the players too when I say we are all grateful to you. I hope you enjoy the Official Arsenal Annual 2008.

Thanks again,

Arsène Wenger

Message from the Manager

Dawn of a new era

Arsenal

The Club entered a brave new era with the move to Emirates Stadium. How would they fare in their first Premiership campaign at their new home?

AUGUST

⚽ A new season, a new strip, the first Premiership match at Emirates Stadium and Theo Walcott's Arsenal debut: it was 'in with the new' all-round when Aston Villa came to North London in August. However, the day almost ended in disaster when Olof Mellberg opened the scoring nine minutes into the second half. Fortunately, Gilberto – who was fantastic all afternoon – grabbed an equaliser seven minutes from time.

Robin van Persie on the attack at Manchester City

▶ Tomas Rosicky made his Premiership debut for the Gunners in the away game at Manchester City but he and his team-mates left the City Of Manchester Stadium empty-handed. Thierry Henry and Robin van Persie came close with a host of chances to score but it was Joey Barton's first-half penalty which separated the sides. This was the first time that City had beaten the Gunners in 19 matches between the teams.

Thierry Henry tucks away a penalty

> **"WE WILL QUICKLY START TO WIN THESE SORT OF GAMES BUT WE ARE NOT QUITE READY PHYSICALLY AT THE MOMENT."**

⚽ After a disappointing opening month, Arsenal needed to get their Premiership campaign back on track in September – and they did.

However, the first match of the month ended in another 1–1 draw. Middlesbrough were the visitors to Emirates Stadium and they took the lead through James Morrison in the 22nd minute. Arsenal captain Henry levelled the score with a penalty in the 67th minute. Debutants Julio Baptista and William Gallas both came close to netting a winner.

Where better to win your first Premiership tie of the season than Old Trafford? Arsène Wenger's boys did just that when they utterly dominated the match against Manchester United. Cesc Fabregas put in perhaps his finest performance to date and Emmanuel Adebayor scored the winner four minutes from time. Praise too for Jens Lehmann who made a sensational save from Ole Gunnar Solksjaer just moments after Adebayor's goal.

Don't let the 3–0 scoreline from the encounter with Sheffield United fool you; the Gunners had to really work to beat the Blades. This was a physical and determined performance from Neil Warnock's men. However, once Gallas had opened the scoring in the 63rd minute, Arsenal were on course for victory.

A wonder goal from van Persie secured all three points at The Valley. Charlton Athletic had actually gone ahead in the 21st minute but two goals from the Dutchman – with that special strike coming in the second half – sent the points to North London.

ELEMENTARY MY DEAR ARSENAL

Arsène Wenger has a Yorkshire Terrier dog called Lilly.

Robin celebrates his wonder goal at The Valley

19 AUGUST 2006 ARSENAL **1-1** ASTON VILLA (GILBERTO 83)
26 AUGUST 2006 MANCHESTER CITY **1-0** ARSENAL
9 SEPTEMBER 2006 ARSENAL **1-1** MIDDLESBROUGH (HENRY 67 PEN)
17 SEPTEMBER 2006 MANCHESTER UNITED **0-1** ARSENAL (ADEBAYOR 86)
23 SEPTEMBER 2006 ARSENAL **3-0** SHEFFIELD UNITED
(GALLAS 63, JAGIELKA OG 69, HENRY 80)
30 SEPTEMBER 2006 CHARLTON ATHLETIC **1-2** ARSENAL
(VAN PERSIE 32, 50)

PREMIERSHIP
Season Report

⚽ The Gunners continued this improved form in October, claiming seven points from a possible nine.

Arsène Wenger celebrated 10 years at the Club before the kick-off against Watford and his team made sure the celebrations continued into the night. The Gunners' fourth successive league win came thanks to goals from Thierry Henry and Emmanuel Adebayor, after an own goal from Jordan Stewart. Further good news came in the shape of Gael Clichy's return after a lengthy injury lay-off.

Henry opened the scoring in the opening minute at the Madejski Stadium and the Gunners ran out as 4–0 winners over Reading. Henry also netted a penalty and the other goalscorers were Alexander

Cesc Fabregas on the ball at Reading

Hleb and Robin van Persie. This match was played on Arsène Wenger's 57th birthday. Many happy returns, Mr Wenger!

Van Persie's stunning free-kick against Everton was worthy of being a match-winner but was actually an equaliser in a 1–1 draw. The Gunners had dominated the match but were unable to convert more than one chance.

RIGHT: The wondrous Walcott

14 OCTOBER 2006 ARSENAL 3–0 WATFORD
(STEWART OG 33, HENRY 43, ADEBAYOR 66)
22 OCTOBER 2006 READING 0–4 ARSENAL
(HENRY 1, 70 (PEN), HLEB 39, VAN PERSIE 49)
28 OCTOBER 2006 ARSENAL 1–1 EVERTON (VAN PERSIE 70)
5 NOVEMBER 2006 WEST HAM UNITED 1–0 ARSENAL
12 NOVEMBER 2006 ARSENAL 3–0 LIVERPOOL
(FLAMINI 41, TOURE 56, GALLAS 88)
18 NOVEMBER 2006 NEWCASTLE UNITED 1–1 ARSENAL (HENRY 70)
25 NOVEMBER 2006 BOLTON WANDERERS 3–1 ARSENAL (GILBERTO 45)
29 NOVEMBER 2006 FULHAM 2–1 ARSENAL (VAN PERSIE 36)

Super-sub Henry scores at Newcastle

⚽ The temperature dropped, the skies grew darker in November and the team's form this month brought little cheer to the fans, aside from a glorious home victory over Liverpool.

A frustrating afternoon at Upton Park looked set to be heading for a 0–0 draw. However, Marlon Harewood's late goal meant the Gunners left East London without even a point to show for their efforts. A week later the Gunners beat Liverpool 3–0 at Emirates Stadium thanks to goals from Mathieu Flamini, Kolo Toure and William Gallas. The home fans roared their appreciation all afternoon.

Cometh the hour, cometh the man and when Arsenal were trailing at half-time against Newcastle United, Wenger sent on Henry to try and rescue something. He did just that with a smashing free-kick in the 70th minute. However, neither he nor a team-mate was able to net a winner.

The Reebok Stadium is proving to be an unpopular venue for everyone associated with Arsenal. A character-building visit there ended with the team losing 3–1. Former Gunner Nicolas Anelka scored two of the home side's goals. Gilberto grabbed the visitors' goal.

Another away trip ended in defeat four days later when Fulham beat Arsenal 2–1 at Craven Cottage. Van Persie scored a breathtaking free-kick in the 36th minute but, by then, the Cottagers had already scored twice. The dismissal of Philippe Senderos did little to help the Gunners' cause and brought to an end a largely difficult month.

It's a goal! Toure nets v Liverpool

ELEMENTARY MY DEAR ARSENAL

EMIRATES DETECTIVE

The club's Brazilian duo enjoy making music: Gilberto plays the mandolin and Denilson plays the Portuguese hand drum! Let's get down to that Salsa beat!

"WHEN YOU SCORE IT'S A VERY POWERFUL EMOTION. SO I WENT TO THE FANS BECAUSE THEY ARE FANTASTIC."

Spot on! Gilberto's penalty v Spurs

strike from the edge of the area. However, Michael Essien equalised seven minutes later and honours were even. A hard-fought and evenly matched evening of Premiership football at Wigan tilted Arsenal's way when Adebayor slotted home Cesc Fabregas's pass in the 88th minute to win the match.

In the first two minutes of the second-half against Portsmouth at Emirates Stadium, the visitors went 2–0 up. However, Arsenal fought back and scored twice in 120 seconds themselves through Adebayor and Gilberto. Adebayor's strike was particularly sweet, converting a fine cross from Theo Walcott.

DECEMBER

⚽ Despite a few disappointments, Arsenal provided plenty of Christmas cheer for their fans during December.

There are few louder cheers in Premiership football than those unleashed by Arsenal fans when their team scores against Tottenham Hotspur. Three of these deafening cheers shook North London as an Emmanuel Adebayor strike and two penalties from Gilberto tied up a wonderful derby win.

The Gunners thought they had tied up victory over Chelsea when Mathieu Flamini scored in the 78th minute at Stamford Bridge. After a one-two with Alexander Hleb, the Frenchman cracked home a fine

Riding Robin!

In the final match before Christmas, Arsenal presented their fans with six goals against Blackburn Rovers. The Gunners had actually gone 1–0 down in the 3rd minute, but a fine afternoon of football ended with Wenger's team winning a thriller 6–2. Gilberto, Hleb, Adebayor, Robin van Persie (twice) and Flamini all scored. On Boxing Day, Arsenal beat Watford 2–1 at Vicarage Road. Gilberto nodded the visitors ahead and, after the Hornets equalised, van Persie secured three points seven minutes from time.

The 1–0 defeat at Bramall Lane was a surprise but overall December had been a very decent month for Arsenal in the Premiership. How would they fare in 2007?

2 DECEMBER 2006 ARSENAL **3-0** TOTTENHAM HOTSPUR
(ADEBAYOR 28, GILBERTO 42 PEN, 72 PEN)
10 DECEMBER 2006 CHELSEA **1-1** ARSENAL (FLAMINI 79)
13 DECEMBER 2006 WIGAN ATHLETIC **0-1** ARSENAL (ADEBAYOR 88)
16 DECEMBER 2006 ARSENAL **2-2** PORTSMOUTH
(ADEBAYOR 58, GILBERTO 60)
23 DECEMBER 2006 ARSENAL **6-2** BLACKBURN ROVERS
(GILBERTO 18, HLEB 23, ADEBAYOR 27, VAN PERSIE 85, 88, FLAMINI 90)
26 DECEMBER 2006 WATFORD **1-2** ARSENAL (GILBERTO 19, VAN PERSIE 83)
30 DECEMBER 2006 SHEFFIELD UNITED **1-0** ARSENAL
2 JANUARY 2007 ARSENAL **4-0** CHARLTON ATHLETIC
(HENRY 30 PEN, HOYTE 45, VAN PERSIE 76 PEN, 90)
13 JANUARY 2007 BLACKBURN ROVERS **0-2** ARSENAL (TOURE 37, HENRY 71)
21 JANUARY 2007 ARSENAL **2-1** MANCHESTER UNITED
(VAN PERSIE 83, HENRY 90)

JANUARY

Justin time! Hoyte celebrates his first Arsenal goal

The Charlton victory was hugely satisfying but 11 days later an even more enjoyable victory came in the early evening Saturday match at Ewood Park. Gilberto was sent off just 12 minutes into the proceedings but goals from Kolo Toure and Henry sealed

victory for the Gunners. Henry's goal was magnificent: after a fine run he swapped passes with Fabregas before unleashing a curling shot.

Eight days later, Manchester United came to Emirates Stadium and left pointless after Arsenal beat them 2–1. Many thought that United would emerge winners when Wayne Rooney scored in the 53rd minute. However, with the visitors tiring in the final 10 minutes, goals from van Persie and Henry snatched all three points for Arsenal.

⚽ A 100 per cent Premiership record including another victory over Manchester United – January was a jolly time for the Arsenal faithful.

Thierry Henry's return from injury had been eagerly awaited and, when he did come back, he was the architect of a comprehensive victory over Charlton Athletic. Opening the scoring after half an hour with a penalty, he was joined on the score-sheet by Justin Hoyte and van Persie, who netted twice. A good victory, then, but in truth the scoreline could have been far more emphatic.

Team spirit as the Gunners win again

ELEMENTARY MY DEAR ARSENAL

EMIRATES DETECTIVE

Former Gunner Thierry Henry is an international ambassador for Tommy Hilfiger and Freddie Ljungberg has modelled for Calvin Klein

PREMIERSHIP
SEASON REPORT

⚽ Why should you never leave a football match early? Arsenal provided the answer in February.

Arsenal have enjoyed a fantastic record against Middlesbrough in recent years and, until the 64th minute of their match at the Riverside Stadium, they were again dominating proceedings. However, Phillippe Senderos was sent off and Yakubu Aiyegbeni scored from the resultant penalty. A goal down away from home and reduced to 10 men – what would Arsenal do?

They would dig in and fight for a result of course! In their previous league match, the Gunners had secured all three points at the end of the match against Manchester United. This time, they secured a valuable point late on when Thierry Henry sent a fine shot into the far corner of the net.

Eight days later, Wigan Athletic were the vistors to Emirates Stadium and it was another late, late show from Wenger's team. Danny Landzaat gave the visitors the lead 10 minutes before half-time and held onto their lead until the 81st minute, by which time radio commentators were beginning to predict that Wigan would be the first team to beat the Gunners at their new home.

Then Fitz Hall scored an own goal when he connected with Mathieu Flamini's cross. Having levelled the score, Arsenal went one better and won the tie when Tomas Rosicky powered home a fine header. It was drama, it was victory, it was Arsenal.

Rosicky scored a late winner against Wigan

Henry equalises at 'Boro

ELEMENTARY MY DEAR ARSENAL

EMIRATES DETECTIVE

Emirates Stadium includes a Guide Dog toilet near the North Bridge. Arsenal is the first club to provide such a service to the mutts that accompany blind and visually-impaired supporters!

⚽ March was a month of two halves for the Gunners – they experienced the sugar-sweet rush of victory on two occasions and then tasted the bitterness of defeat twice.

The happy half of the month kicked off at home against Reading with a line-up depleted by injury. Both goals came in the second half, and both were dispatched by a Brazilian. First up was a penalty converted by Gilberto, awarded after Gael Clichy had been fouled in the box. Then, Julio Baptista collected a pass from Denilson, beat his man and poked the ball home.

The next three points came at Villa Park where Arsenal moved to third in the Premiership thanks to Abou Diaby's 10th minute goal. The shot had actually come in from Baptista, but Diaby unwittingly deflected it past Thomas Sorensen to give Wenger's men an early edge. Despite creating a raft of further chances, the Gunners did not add to the scoring. Neither, though, did they concede.

Then came a pair of visits to Merseyside both of which ended in defeat. First up was the game at Everton, before which Arsène Wenger had singled out Andy

Johnson for praise. The striker confirmed Wenger's words when he lashed home a last-minute winner.

Having beaten Liverpool at Anfield in both the FA Cup and Carling Cup this season, Arsenal hoped to complete a treble in the Premiership. However, a Peter Crouch hat-trick fuelled a thumping defeat for the Gunners. William Gallas briefly gave Arsenal hope at 3–1, but a fourth Liverpool goal soon followed.

MARCH

> "THE AIM IS TO GET AS HIGH AS WE CAN AFTER BEATING ASTON VILLA. WE ARE A BIT FAR FROM CHELSEA AT THE MOMENT BUT WE HOPE AT LEAST TO STAY HERE IN THIRD AND MAYBE WE CAN CLIMB A POSITION."

Gallas grabbed a goal at Anfield

3 FEBRUARY 2007 MIDDLESBROUGH **1-1** ARSENAL (HENRY 77)
11 FEBRUARY 2007 ARSENAL **2-1** WIGAN ATHLETIC
(HALL OG 81, ROSICKY 85)
3 MARCH 2007 ARSENAL **2-1** READING
(GILBERTO 51, BAPTISTA 62)
14 MARCH 2007 ASTON VILLA **0-1** ARSENAL (DIABY 10)
18 MARCH 2007 EVERTON **1-0** ARSENAL
31 MARCH 2007 LIVERPOOL **4-1** ARSENAL (GALLAS 74)

PREMIERSHIP
SEASON REPORT

APRIL

⚽ With three wins, two draws and one defeat, April was a month that reflected Arsenal's entire 2006–07 Premiership campaign: plenty of positives but not quite enough points to mount a title challenge.

The defeat came in the first match of the month as West Ham United became the first visitors to win at Emirates Stadium. It was amazing that the Gunners lost as they utterly dominated the match and peppered visiting goalkeeper Robert Green with shots. On Easter Monday, Arsène Wenger's men took a point from a tight match at St James Park and remained in fourth place.

Cesc's soaring celebration!

Former Gunner Nicolas Anelka gave Bolton an early lead at Emirates Stadium but goals from Tomas Rosicky and Cesc Fabregas ensured a home victory. It was the Spaniard's first goal for a year and his cool finish was greeted with ecstasy by him, his team-mates and supporters. He and Rosicky were again among the goals as Arsenal beat Manchester City 3–1. Julio Baptista swept home the third after great work from Alexander Hleb.

And so to White Hart Lane where substitute Fabregas looked to have inspired Arsenal to victory with Kolo Toure and Emmanuel Adebayor both netting. However, a last-minute strike from Jermaine Jenas ensured that honours remained even on the day. The month ended with a victory over struggling Fulham. After Simon Davies had cancelled out Baptista's opener, Adebayor and Gilberto scored in the closing stages to confirm victory.

Baptista nets v Manchester City

16

7 APRIL 2007 ARSENAL 0-1 WEST HAM UNITED
9 APRIL 2007 NEWCASTLE UNITED 0-0 ARSENAL
14 APRIL 2007 ARSENAL 2-1 BOLTON WANDERERS
(ROSICKY 31, FABREGAS 46)
17 APRIL 2007 ARSENAL 3-1 MANCHESTER CITY
(ROSICKY 12, FABREGAS 73, BAPTISTA 80)
21 APRIL 2007 TOTTENHAM HOTSPUR 2-2 ARSENAL
(TOURE 64, ADEBAYOR 78)
29 APRIL 2007 ARSENAL 3-1 FULHAM
(BAPTISTA 4, ADEBAYOR 84, GILBERTO 87 PEN)
6 MAY 2007 ARSENAL 1-1 CHELSEA (GILBERTO, 43 PEN)
13 MAY 2007 PORTSMOUTH 0-0 ARSENAL

⚽ With a top-four finish in the Premiership assured, Arsenal finished all-square with their two Premiership opponents in May. In doing so, the Gunners played a direct role in the destiny of the Premiership crown – though not quite in the way they'd hoped at the start of the campaign.

Chelsea arrived at Emirates Stadium with their grasp on the Premiership trophy looking distinctly loose. That grasp loosened even further when, two minutes before the break, Khalid Boulahrouz fouled Julio Baptista in the area. The defender was sent off and Gilberto scored from the spot. Could Chelsea, who needed victory to keep their title hopes alive, rescue themselves in the second half? Almost. Michael Essien scored in the 70th minute but it was the Gunners who finished strongest, with Emmanuel Eboue rattling the crossbar at the close. This result sent the Premiership trophy to Old Trafford.

"A LOT OF PEOPLE WERE TELLING ME I WAS GOING TO SCORE IN THIS GAME AGAINST BOLTON, INCLUDING ROBIN VAN PERSIE. HE TOLD ME 'TODAY YOU'RE GOING TO SCORE CESC' "

The final match of the campaign came at Portsmouth where Julio Baptista had two great chances to break the deadlock but failed to convert either. The first came from the penalty spot in the 41st minute but David James saved the Brazilian's effort. Then, the Beast failed to take full advantage of a free header. In addition, Alexander Hleb hit the side-netting and one of Pompey's former Gunners, Nwankwo Kanu, forced a fine save from Mart Poom. A tame affair ended 0–0.

A fourth-place finish was disappointing for the Gunners fans, but given the injuries the squad suffered, it was an admirable achievement. Their home and away fixtures against the other top four sides brought three wins, two draws and just one defeat. With a little more consistency next season, this young Arsenal side could be the team to beat.

MAY

Left: Gael Clichy holds off a challenge from Portsmouth's Gary O'Neill

Below: Gilberto sends Cech the wrong way and the Premiership title to Old Trafford

ELEMENTARY MY DEAR ARSENAL

Gilberto played in every minute of Brazil's winning World Cup campaign in 2002

EMIRATES DETECTIVE

17

FA CUP

Settling some scores

Arsenal

Arsenal's FA Cup campaign began with a fantastic victory at Anfield, continued with a much longed-for defeat of Bolton Wanderers but concluded with a dramatic defeat at Ewood Park.

Here are the highs and lows of a hard-fought campaign...

Toure trumps the Trotters

THIRD ROUND

⚽ AWAY V LIVERPOOL

Two fantastic late first-half Tomas Rosicky strikes were the highlights of this satisfying start to the FA Cup campaign. Midway through the second half, Dirk Kuyt pulled one back but, seven minutes from time, Thierry Henry cut in from the left and fired past Jerzy Dudek to make it 3–1 for the visitors. Victory at Anfield is always special and this was a sweet start to the Club's FA Cup campaign.

Match Fact: This was Manuel Almunia's first match since November's league clash with Liverpool.

FOURTH ROUND

⚽ HOME V BOLTON WANDERERS

When the visitors went 1–0 ahead after 50 minutes of this match, many believed that Arsenal were about to suffer another defeat by the dreaded Bolton Wanderers. However, the Gunners had different ideas. With 12 minutes remaining, Kolo Toure headed home a Cesc Fabregas free-kick. It ended all square and a trip to the Reebok was on the cards.

Match Fact: This was the third match in seven days that saw Arsenal recover after falling behind – the first two were against Manchester United and Tottenham.

REPLAY

⚽ AWAY V BOLTON WANDERERS

Last season, Bolton dumped the Gunners out of the FA Cup in a fourth-round tie at the Reebok Stadium. This season, Arsenal returned the compliment. Emmanuel Adebayor's early goal looked set to win the tie, but the home side equalised at the death. In extra time, Freddie Ljungberg restored Arsenal's lead and another goal from Adebayor meant the Gunners were through, despite having missed two penalties. It was an action-packed night and Arsenal ended on top.

Match Fact: This was Freddie's first match after two months out with a hamstring injury.

You were saying? Thierry celebrates at Anfield

18

How did that stay out?
Frustration v Blackburn Rovers

⚽ HOME V BLACKBURN ROVERS

Thanks to a fixture pile-up this came just three days after the drama at the Reebok, but this was a less eventful tie. Rovers were in resolute mood and none more so than Brad Friedel who put in a vintage performance. His double-save from Henry and Hoyte in the second half was particularly memorable. Another replay beckoned...

✎ **Match Fact:** This was Arsenal's first domestic 0–0 draw for 56 games.

Kolo Toure's brother Yaya is a professional footballer who plays for Barcelona. They are both established internationals for the Côte d' Ivoire

ELEMENTARY MY DEAR ARSENAL

EMIRATES DETECTIVE

I can't here you? Manu cups his ear in the Cup

⚽ AWAY V BLACKBURN ROVERS

Having won several games this season with late, late goals Arsenal were on the wrong end of such a moment when Benni McCarthy lashed home the winner in the 87th minute. The Gunners could justifiably feel aggrieved at their defeat because they had created the best chances of the game. Julio Baptista could have scored a hat-trick and Freddie Ljungberg had a convincing appeal for a penalty turned down. However, the Gunners did not turn chances into goals and therefore went out of the Cup.

✎ **Match Fact:** A total of nine first-teamers were unavailable for this match.

THIRD ROUND, 6 JANUARY 2007
LIVERPOOL **1–3** ARSENAL (ROSICKY 37, 45 HENRY 84)
FOURTH ROUND, 28 JANUARY 2007
ARSENAL **1–1** BOLTON WANDERERS (TOURE 78)
FOUTH ROUND REPLAY, 14 FEBRUARY 2007
BOLTON WANDERERS **1–3** ARSENAL
(ADEBAYOR 13, 120 LJUNGBERG 109)
FIFTH ROUND, 17 FEBRUARY 2007
ARSENAL **0–0** BLACKBURN ROVERS
FIFTH ROUND REPLAY, 28 FEBRUARY 2007
BLACKBURN ROVERS **1–0** ARSENAL

CHAMPIONS LEAGUE
SEASON REPORT
The European tour
The UEFA Champions League proved to be as exciting
and challenging as ever for the Gunners. Here is the full story of their march through the qualifying round and the group stage...

Arsenal

QUALIFYING ROUND

⚽ DINAMO ZAGREB V ARSENAL

Arsenal grabbed a significant advantage in the first leg of this tie with three cracking goals. Two of them came from Cesc Fabregas and the other was scored by Robin van Persie. Pick of the bunch was the Spaniard's second which came at the end of a fine, weaving run.

Euro Fact: This was Cesc's 100th appearance for Arsenal.

⚽ ARSENAL V DINAMO ZAGREB

The visitors took a 12th-minute lead in this second leg, with a goal from Eduardo da Silva (now of Arsenal fame). It shook the Gunners right into action. Van Persie terrorised the opposition defence and it is a surprise that he did not score. However, he did provide the cross for Freddie Ljungberg's headed goal. The winner was scored by Mathieu Flamini and created by Theo Walcott.

Euro Fact: Freddie was Arsenal captain for the first time.

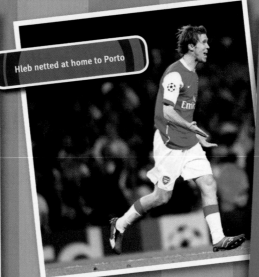

Hleb netted at home to Porto

Dynamism v Dinamo Zagreb

20

GROUP STAGE

⚽ HAMBURG V ARSENAL

A Tomas Rosicky wonder goal proved to be the moment that separated the sides in Arsenal's first group tie of the campaign. Captain Gilberto fired Arsenal ahead from the penalty spot after 12 minutes. Eight minutes into the second half, van Persie rolled a nice pass into the path of Rosicky who cracked home a fine strike. A late goal from Boubabcar Sango ensured a nervous finish but the three points left Arsenal on top of Group G.

Euro Fact: When Justin Hoyte replaced Kolo Toure, Arsenal had 11 different nationalities on the pitch – a first in the UEFA Champions League.

⚽ ARSENAL V PORTO

Three days prior to this tie, Thierry Henry had met an Emmanuel Eboue cross to score with his head against Sheffield United. A carbon copy of that goal opened the scoring against Porto. This was a majestic Arsenal performance, and the lead was doubled three minutes after the break when Alexander Hleb did justice to some fine interplay between William Gallas and Henry when he stroked the ball home.

Euro Fact: Of Thierry's first 217 goals for Arsenal, only nine have been headers.

⚽ CSKA MOSCOW V ARSENAL

A long trip to Russia, 90 minutes of tough football on a challenging playing surface and no points for Arsenal – this was a joyless encounter. Van Persie, Kolo Toure and Gilberto came close to scoring for the visitors but none came closer than Henry, who had a seemingly valid goal chalked off by the referee at the end. This was a character-building evening for the Gunners. Daniel Carvalho scored the only goal for the hosts in the first half.

Euro Fact: This was the first Champions League group game defeat since being beaten by Bayern Munich during the 2004–05 season.

⚽ ARSENAL V CSKA MOSCOW

Rarely has a side commanded so much possession and created so many opportunities without finding the back of the net. Van Persie, Hleb, Rosicky, Fabregas, Gilberto and Henry might well have had nightmares after this tie, as they all missed good chances to score. Rosicky's open-goal miss was particularly memorable. However, a fine rearguard action meant the Gunners took a clean sheet and therefore a point.

👐 **Euro Fact:** This was the eighth game at Emirates Stadium and the Gunners were yet to lose there.

⚽ ARSENAL V HAMBURG

Just 240 seconds into this tie, the Germans took the lead through Rafael van der Vaart. The Arsenal fans were getting worried that defeat would make things mathematically tricky when they were into their final group tie against Porto. However, goals from van Persie, Emmanuel Eboue and Julio Baptista sent the Gunners back to the top of the Group. Now, all they needed to do was avoid defeat in Porto and they would be in the hat for the knockout stages.

👐 **Euro Fact:** Henry's booking meant he would miss the Porto trip.

⚽ PORTO V ARSENAL

Both sides knew that a draw here would see both of them progress to the knockout stages – and boy did that show in a match lacking any serious entertainment. However, the Gunners did what they needed to do to finish as winners of Group G. Fabregas was particularly impressive. The Spaniard came close to opening the scoring and also fed Hleb with a fine opportunity.

👐 **Euro Fact:** Emmanuel Adebayor played alone in attack in this tie.

Van Persie scores against Hamburg

⚽ PSV EINDHOVEN V ARSENAL

It was Arsène Wenger's 600th game in charge, but his team could not make it '600 of the best' against the Dutch giants and returned to North London experiencing the bitter taste of defeat. Up until Mendez gave the home side the lead in the 67th minute, the visitors had probably had the best of the chances. Rosicky and Henry displayed a good understanding and both had chances to open the scoring. Adebayor and Fabregas also came close. However, the Gunners ended up on the losing side on the night with an uphill battle ahead in the second leg.

👐 **Euro Fact:** Gilberto scored the fastest goal in UEFA Champions League history against PSV on 25 September 2002. He found the net after just 20.07 seconds and Arsenal went on to win the game 4–0.

⚽ ARSENAL V PSV EINDHOVEN

Some 13 minutes into the second half against the Dutch side, the Gunners went ahead thanks to an own goal by Alex. The home crowd roared their delight but, with just seven minutes left, Alex redeemed himself when he headed an equaliser that saw Arsenal go 2–1 behind on aggregate. It was a disappointing and undeserved conclusion to the team's European adventure.

👐 **Euro Fact:** Arsenal conceded only six goals in 10 European ties during the 2006–07 season.

Group G Table	P	W	D	L	F	A	Pts
Arsenal	6	3	2	1	7	3	11
Porto	6	3	2	1	9	4	11
CSKA Moscow	6	2	2	2	4	5	8
Hamburg	6	1	0	5	7	15	3

8 AUGUST 2006 DINAMO ZAGREB **0-3** ARSENAL
(FABREGAS 63, 79, VAN PERSIE 64)
23 AUGUST 2006 ARSENAL **2-1** DINAMO ZAGREB
(LJUNGBERG 77, FLAMINI 90)
13 SEPTEMBER 2006 ARSENAL **2-0** PORTO (HENRY 38, HLEB 48)
17 OCTOBER 2006 CSKA MOSCOW **1-0** ARSENAL
1 NOVEMBER 2006 ARSENAL **0-0** CSKA MOSCOW
21 NOVEMBER 2006 ARSENAL **3-1** HAMBURG
(VAN PERSIE 52, EBOUE 83, BAPTISTA 88)
6 DECEMBER 2006 FC PORTO **0-0** ARSENAL
20 FEBRUARY 2007 PSV EINDHOVEN **1-0** ARSENAL
7 MARCH 2007 ARSENAL **1-1** PSV EINDHOVEN (ALEX OG 58)

CARLING CUP
SEASON REPORT

Young hearts run free
For the past few years manager Arsène Wenger has used the Carling Cup to blood his youngsters. That same formula was used in 2006–07, but with an even better outcome than before.

THIRD ROUND

⚽ AWAY V WEST BROMWICH ALBION

Arsenal's march to Cardiff began with a trip to the Midlands to face Championship side West Bromwich Albion. In a young Gunners line-up, Jeremie Aliadiere – aged 23 years, 207 days – was the oldest outfield player and he scored in each half to wrap up a fine win for the visitors.

Not that the home side were a pushover. Indeed, Albion started the match in determined fashion and the Gunners had to weather a stormy opening 15 minutes. With former Gunner John Hartson in their ranks, their opponents were potent in attack and Phillipe Senderos and Johan Djourou had to work hard to keep a clean sheet. In the end, Wenger's wonderboys prevailed thanks to Aliadiere's goals. In a side containing nine teenagers, four players made their debuts including Denilson and Mark Randall.

FOURTH ROUND

⚽ AWAY V EVERTON

Full of incident and goalmouth action, this was a cracking cup tie which Arsenal won with a late goal from Emmanuel Adebayor. Wenger's young side did not so much sail into the last eight of the Carling Cup as battle their way there. The Toffeemen had held Arsenal at Emirates Stadium in the Premiership a few weeks earlier. This time, the Gunners prevailed.

Everton had a player sent off in the 19th minute and during the break Mart Poom replaced Manuel Almunia, who had suffered a head injury. There was end-to-end action all night with Adebayor, Aliadiere and Theo Walcott all coming close to scoring. However, it was Adebayor who netted the winner, converting a fine corner from Mathieu Flamini with five minutes left.

Take that! Manu heads the winner at Everton

A Baptista of fire for Liverpool

LEFT: Walcott goes West

EMIRATES DETECTIVE

ELEMENTARY MY DEAR ARSENAL

The Control Room is on Club Level in the Orange Quadrant. It is fitted with an attendance ticker from which staff can view the flow of fans entering the Stadium!

22

Rosicky sends Arsenal to the Final

⚽ AWAY V LIVERPOOL

In one of the season's most memorable matches, Wenger's young Gunners grew in stature as they prevailed in a nine-goal thriller at Anfield. This was the first time in nearly 77 years that Liverpool had conceded six goals at home. A hectic and heady opening 45 minutes saw Robbie Fowler cancel out Aliadiere's opener. In the last five minutes before the break, two Julio Baptista goals and one from Alexandre Song gave Arsenal a 4–1 lead.

In the second half, Baptista scored twice more and missed a penalty before full-time. Steven Gerrard and Sami Hyypia netted consolation goals. "You'll never walk alone," sang the home fans faithfully. As for the young Gunners, they had never walked taller. Could they take this fine form into the semi-final against local rivals Spurs?

⚽ AWAY V TOTTENHAM HOTSPUR

Such had been the heroics of the young Gunners in reaching the semi-final that many were waiting for them to fail – not least the Tottenham fans. Those fans were on cloud nine when a Julio Baptista own-goal doubled the lead that Dimitar Berbatov had already given the home side. But don't ever doubt the Beast...

In the second half, with some Spurs fans already planning their trip to Cardiff, Baptista scored twice to give Arsenal the edge. First, he played a fine one-two with Walcott and beat Paul Robinson. Then he met a fine cross from Justin Hoyte to level the score. There was still time for Cesc Fabregas and Walcott to come close to a winner. The Gunners ended the tie on a high, but could they confirm that high by finishing off the job at Emirates Stadium the following week?

⚽ HOME V TOTTENHAM HOTSPUR

At last! A home Carling Cup tie for Arsenal! It is another measure of the achievement of the young Guns that they only played one tie at home on the way to Cardiff. And what a tie it proved to be. Emmanuel Adebayor converted Tomas Rosicky's pass to give Arsenal the lead. However, Spurs equalised late on to send the tie into extra-time. In the 105th minute, Aliadiere was again the hero for Arsenal when he capitalised on a Spurs mistake and lashed the ball into the corner of the net.

Arsenal's place in the Final was confirmed when Rosicky's shot bounced off Pascal Chimbonda into his own net. What pride the supporters felt in the heroics of the young Arsenal side that reached the Carling Cup final. It is to be hoped that they felt just as much pride themselves.

Hitting new Hoytes!

THIRD ROUND, 24 OCTOBER 2006
WEST BROMWICH ALBION **0-2** ARSENAL
(ALIADIERE 34 PEN, 50)
FOURTH ROUND, 8 NOVEMBER 2006
EVERTON **0-1** ARSENAL (ADEBAYOR 85)
QUARTER-FINAL, 9 JANUARY 2007
LIVERPOOL **3-6** ARSENAL
(ALIADIERE 27, BAPTISTA 40, 45, 60, 84, SONG 45)
SEMI-FINAL FIRST LEG, 24 JANUARY 2007
TOTTENHAM HOTSPUR **2-2** ARSENAL (BAPTISTA 64, 77)
SEMI-FINAL SECONND LEG, 31 JANUARY 2007
ARSENAL **3-1** TOTTENHAM HOTSPUR
(ADEBAYOR 77, ALIADIERE 105, CHIMBONDA 113 OG)

CARLING CUP

SEASON REPORT

Boy Wonders!

An extraordinary afternoon of football saw the young Gunners give the Chelsea first-team a real fright in the Carling Cup Final. Rarely has a defeated team been able to draw more pride from a performance. Here, we take a look back at a memorable afternoon.

Arsenal

FINAL

⚽ One of the most eventful cup finals in Arsenal's history might have ended with the Gunners on the losing side, but it won Arsène Wenger's young stars a host of new admirers. For anyone who was not already aware of the exciting prospects in the Arsenal ranks, this game would have been an incredible eye-opener.

The Gunners started the match in blistering form and Chelsea seemed stunned in the opening stages as the boys in red and white dominated the proceedings while playing superb, pacy, penetrating football.

▲ This was reflected when they took the lead in the 12th minute. Theo Walcott collected a clearance and laid off the ball to Abou Diaby, who returned the ball to the advancing Walcott. He quickly curled a beautiful shot past Petr Cech. What a way to open his goalscoring account for the Gunners.

Up, up and away!

Theo opens the scoring in style

24

► After the goal, Arsenal continued to stun Chelsea. Could the young Gunners – with an average age among their outfield players of just 21 – beat the Chelsea first team? In the 21st minute, their efforts to achieve that feat were dealt a blow when Didier Drogba collected a fine pass from Michael Ballack and lashed home an equaliser. However, the Gunners recovered from this setback and continued to test Cech, with Diaby and Julio Baptista having particularly fine efforts brilliantly saved.

The game was held up for six minutes in the second half due to a terrifying injury to John Terry. He attempted a diving header, just as Diaby was clearing the ball from the Arsenal six-yard box, and was accidentally kicked in the head. Terry was stretchered off to warm and respectful applause from all the spectators. When the game resumed, both managers made substitutions and the drama continued to unfurl. Drogba put Chelsea ahead when he headed home Arjen Robben's cross and Arsenal now had their work cut out to get back into the game.

"WE MISSED OUR CHANCE BUT WE ARE FULL OF HOPE. I'M VERY PROUD OF THE PERFORMANCE OF MY TEAM.."

The task became harder for the Gunners when were reduced to nine men, against Chelsea's ten. However, the three red cards should not overshadow what was an exhilarating afternoon of football. Neither should Arsenal's defeat overshadow a superb Carling Cup campaign by Wenger's wonderful youngsters.

The boys done well.

JB leaves JT trailing

Diaby was dynamic!

ELEMENTARY MY DEAR ARSENAL

Mathieu Flamini is friends with French rugby union star Thomas Castaignede, who plays for Watford-based Saracens

EMIRATES DETECTIVE

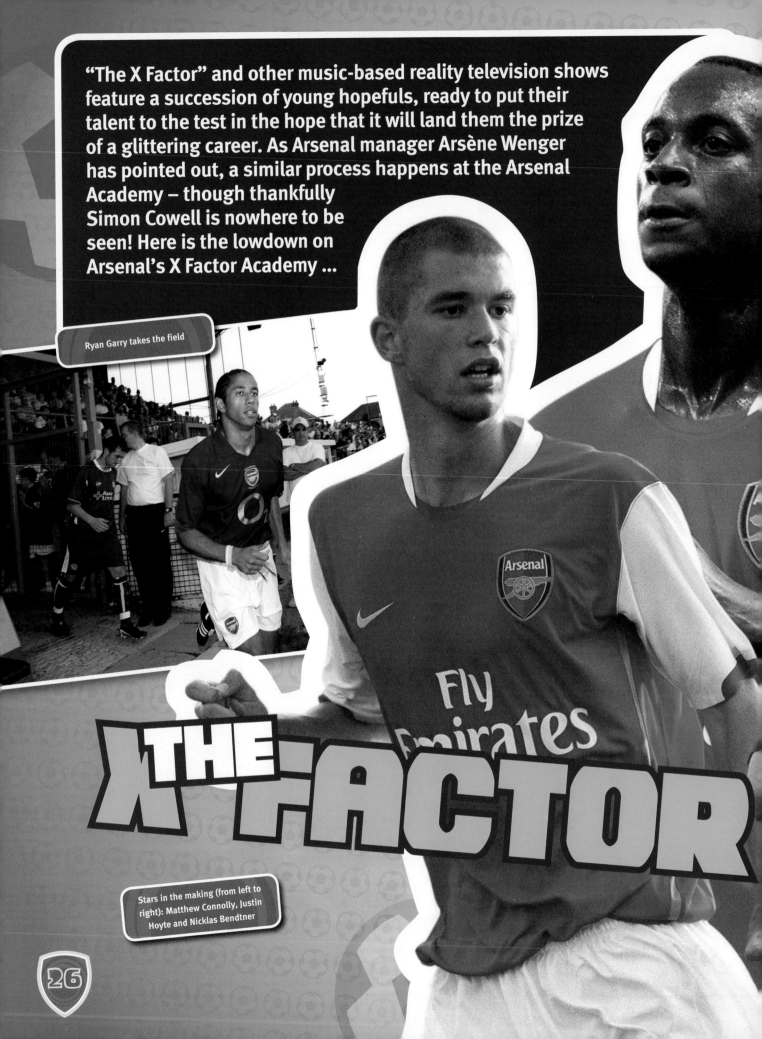

"The X Factor" and other music-based reality television shows feature a succession of young hopefuls, ready to put their talent to the test in the hope that it will land them the prize of a glittering career. As Arsenal manager Arsène Wenger has pointed out, a similar process happens at the Arsenal Academy – though thankfully Simon Cowell is nowhere to be seen! Here is the lowdown on Arsenal's X Factor Academy ...

Ryan Garry takes the field

THE X FACTOR

Stars in the making (from left to right): Matthew Connolly, Justin Hoyte and Nicklas Bendtner

26

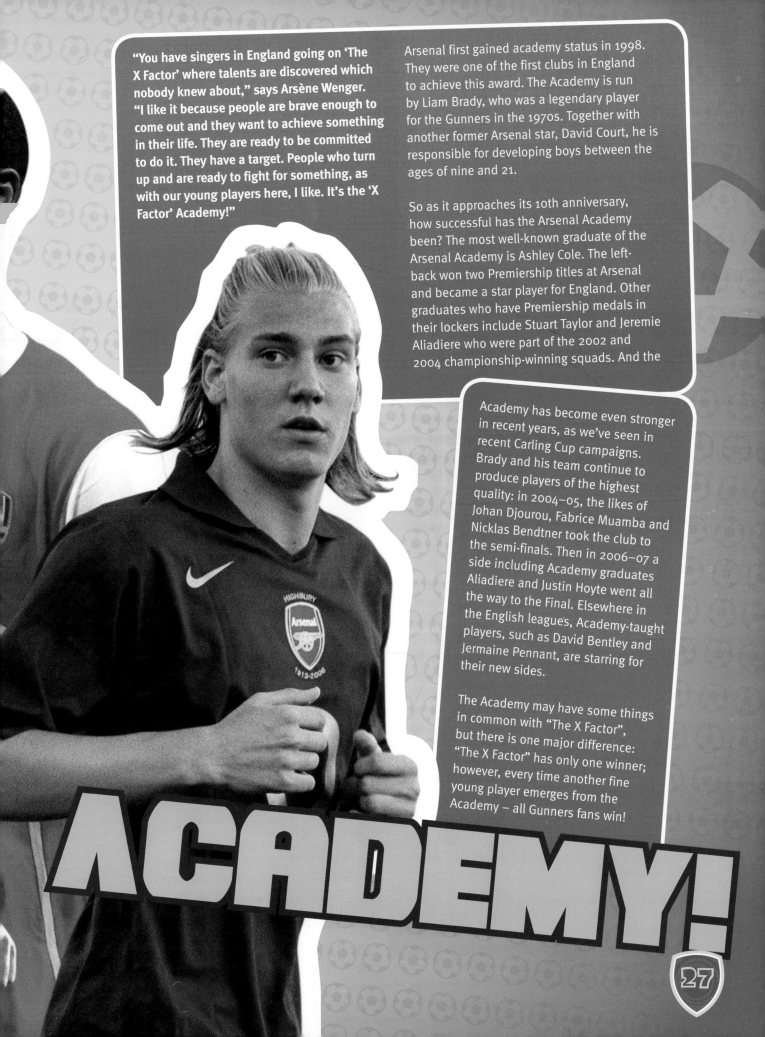

"You have singers in England going on 'The X Factor' where talents are discovered which nobody knew about," says Arsène Wenger. "I like it because people are brave enough to come out and they want to achieve something in their life. They are ready to be committed to do it. They have a target. People who turn up and are ready to fight for something, as with our young players here, I like. It's the 'X Factor' Academy!"

Arsenal first gained academy status in 1998. They were one of the first clubs in England to achieve this award. The Academy is run by Liam Brady, who was a legendary player for the Gunners in the 1970s. Together with another former Arsenal star, David Court, he is responsible for developing boys between the ages of nine and 21.

So as it approaches its 10th anniversary, how successful has the Arsenal Academy been? The most well-known graduate of the Arsenal Academy is Ashley Cole. The left-back won two Premiership titles at Arsenal and became a star player for England. Other graduates who have Premiership medals in their lockers include Stuart Taylor and Jeremie Aliadiere who were part of the 2002 and 2004 championship-winning squads. And the

Academy has become even stronger in recent years, as we've seen in recent Carling Cup campaigns. Brady and his team continue to produce players of the highest quality: in 2004–05, the likes of Johan Djourou, Fabrice Muamba and Nicklas Bendtner took the club to the semi-finals. Then in 2006–07 a side including Academy graduates Aliadiere and Justin Hoyte went all the way to the Final. Elsewhere in the English leagues, Academy-taught players, such as David Bentley and Jermaine Pennant, are starring for their new sides.

The Academy may have some things in common with "The X Factor", but there is one major difference: "The X Factor" has only one winner; however, every time another fine young player emerges from the Academy – all Gunners fans win!

ACADEMY!

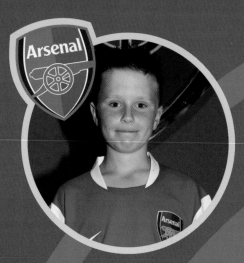

MASCOT FOR THE DAY

It is surely every Junior Gunner's dream to be the club mascot on a match day. And for Todd his dream came true on Sunday, 29 April when Arsenal played Fulham at Emirates Stadium. Now follow the young gun as his big day unfolds.

Todd and his dad arrive at Emirates Stadium well before the kick-off.

Yeah, Dad, Don't make a fuss!

Looking forward to it, son?

Hello, Sue. Nice to meet you.

Hi, Todd. Welcome to Emirates Stadium. I'm Sue Campbell, and I'm going to be looking after you today.

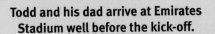

Try this on for size.

Then there are more introductions ...

I'm Gunnersaurus. You may recognise me. There aren't too many seven-foot tall, green fellas about the place!

28

junior GUNNERS

Arsenal

Once again, the greatest supporters' club in football has had a fantastic year. Here are just some of the highlights ...

Fantastic Forum!

The second Junior Gunners forum was held and the special guests were Theo Walcott and Justin Hoyte. An e-newsletter was sent to all the Junior Gunners asking for their questions. The 100 JGs who sent the most imaginative questions were invited along to ask Justin and Theo in person! The questions included: if you where on a desert island what luxury item would you take with you? and football-related questions too.

Christmas Party

The first ever Junior Gunners Christmas Party to be held at Emirates Stadium was a roaring success. The Junior Gunners got to watch the players train on the pitch, and then Gunnersaurus turned up and fired prizes into the crowd from his canon. The young fans wore party masks, got to meet first-team players and generally had a day to remember for ever.

Ken Banham Tournament

The 2007 Ken Banham Tournament took place on Sunday 9 April. Arsenal's Hale End Academy hosted the tournament and the event proved to be an absolute corker! Nineteen teams entered and the winners were Ashe Athletic who beat Tunbridge Wells in the final 4–1 on penalties to take the trophy. The rules for entering the tournament are that each team must have seven players, all players must be aged 12 and under, and one player of the team must be a current Junior Gunner member.

Membership Benefits

There are so many reasons to join the Junior Gunners. Here are just a few ...

- You could be selected to watch the first-team train on the annual members' day.
- You might be photographed with the entire first-team squad at the annual photo-call.
- You get the opportunity to go on Junior Gunners trips.
- You can enter exclusive competitions.
- You get the chance to become ballboy/girl.
- You get the oppportunity to win a Junior Gunner Award and collect it from a first-team player..

See the Junior Gunners section on **www.arsenal.com** for full details!

Philippe Senderos and Manuel Almunia in a party mood

Theo Walcott and Justin Hoyte field questions at the Junior Gunners Forum

31

THE VISIONARIES

HOW HERBERT CHAPMAN AND ARSÈNE WENGER REVOLUTIONISED ARSENAL

Putting us on the map!

Arsenal station, on the Piccadilly Line of London Underground if you didn't know, used to be called Gillespie Road until Chapman convinced the local authorities to change the name following the Club's move north of the river. This was not just a cosmetic move – the presence of the Club's name on the tube map gave it a higher profile and helped draw in more supporters. Arsenal is the only football team in London to have a tube station named after them, and it's all thanks to Herbert Chapman.

Kitted out!

During the 1932–33 season, Chapman noticed someone wearing a red sleeveless jumper over a white shirt and decided this combination of colours would be a good replacement for the previously all-red shirts worn

by the team. He believed it would help the players see each other on the pitch more clearly. The kits were introduced in March 1933 and the Gunners won the title that season. This was not his first moment of kit wizardry. He introduced numbered shirts for the first time in 1928.

There were seven decades between their reigns at the Club but between them Herbert Chapman and Arsène Wenger were as responsible for a host of innovations both at Arsenal and within the game in general. Here we outline the main moments of genius of the two Managers...

Two by two!

For the 1930 FA Cup Final, Arsenal and Huddersfield Town's players emerged from the tunnel side by side. This was the first FA Cup Final where this happened, but it has become a familiar and cherished part of the big day.

Out with the pyramids!

Prior to changes to the offside law in 1925, most football teams had played a 2–3–5 formation. However, after the offside law was changed, Chapman introduced a new 3–2–2–3 formation, which led to a more attacking unit.

Lights!

Chapman was the first manager to advocate the use of floodlights and the use of a white ball to aid visibility. He also came up with the idea of a 10-yard semi-circle on the edge of the penalty box. Chapman also reportedly discussed the idea of artificial playing surfaces being used. All of these ideas subsequently came to fruition in the game.

Top training!

Wenger introduced new training and preparation techniques. He carried a stopwatch and timed to the second every part of the training programmes. He increased and developed the amount of stretching players did and employed masseurs. Wenger also sends players with particularly bad injuries to the south of France for treatment – this worked wonders for Tony Adams and Robert Pires!

Arsenal's fourth FA Cup victory under Wenger came in 2005

Up with the kids!

In 1998, Arsenal became one of the first clubs in England to be awarded Academy status when the Frenchman set up a much-envied Academy which is run by Arsenal legend Liam Brady. The success of the Academy is clear to see now by the incredibly talented young players who make up so much of the first-team squad – many of them are Academy graduates and there's more where they came from!

Herbert Chapman sits proudly with his collection of players...and trophies!

Turning up the heat!

Wenger could be nicknamed "Mr Details". For instance, he arranged for the temperature on the team bus to be raised in order to keep the players' muscles supple. He was the architect of the new Training Centre, and his attention to detail meant he even got involved in selecting the right furniture and cultery!

Thought for food!

During his time managing in Japan, Wenger noticed that the people there have a very healthy diet. He revolutionised the diet of the Arsenal players who found they were dished up meals with boiled chicken, vegetables and rice. Their performances soon improved and other clubs took notice of these developments.

Ground for improvement!

As you sit and stare in awe at the Club's new home, spare a thought for Wenger who was a key advocate of Arsenal moving to a new stadium. He has also been behind many of the features of Emirates Stadium including the size of the pitch, the design and temperature of the dressing rooms and so much more!

ELEMENTARY MY DEAR ARSENAL

EMIRATES DETECTIVE

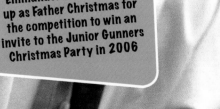

Emmanuel Eboue dressed up as Father Christmas for the competition to win an invite to the Junior Gunners Christmas Party in 2006

THE ASCENT OF ARSENAL

From its humble roots in South London to the magnificent Emirates Stadium, Arsenal Football Club has enjoyed a spectacular history. Oh yes, they've won a few trophies along the way, too. An evolution of excellence, here is the story of the Gunners...

The Woolwich days

One day, some workers at the Royal Arsenal in Woolwich had a bright idea: let's form a football team! They called it Dial Square, named after one of the Arsenal's workshops. The team were given a set of red shirts but changed their name a few times, first to Woolwich Reds, then to Royal Arsenal and then to Woolwich Arsenal. In 1893 they joined the Football League. Woolwich Arsenal's first League match was against Newcastle United and it ended in a 2–2 draw.

1900s–1930s

In 1913, Arsenal moved from south London to Highbury Stadium. After World War I, the word Woolwich was dropped from the club name, making it simply Arsenal. Herbert Chapman became the club's eighth manager in 1925 and soon won Arsenal their first major trophies: the FA Cup in 1930 and the League championship in 1931. Arsenal were crowned champions again in 1933, ending up winning five League titles in the 1930s. Glorious times!

1940s–1960s

The Gunners were for some time regularly in the hunt for honours, winning the League championship in 1948 and 1953 and the FA Cup in 1950, courtesy of a 2–0 victory over Liverpool. The 1953 League championship came on goal average after a 3–2 victory over Burnley.

WALLY HARDINGE

ALEX JAMES

JOE MERCER

1970s–1980s

A trophyless run of 17 seasons followed, until Arsenal won the European Fairs Cup in 1970. Then, in 1971, the Gunners completed their first double when Charlie George netted an extra-time winner against Liverpool at Wembley. Arsenal returned to Wembley eight years later to lift the FA Cup again, this time after a dramatic 3–2 victory over Manchester United.

1980s–1990s

George Graham, a member of the 1971 double-winning team, became manager in 1986. In just eight years, Arsenal won two League championships, the Football League Cup twice, the FA Cup and the European Cup-Winners' Cup. Highbury became an all-seater stadium in the 1990s. Arsène Wenger became manager in November 1996, and won the double in his first full season in charge. He was behind the construction of a brand new state-of-the-art training centre. The dressing-room, meanwhile, became home to stars from around the world.

2000s

After three seasons as runners-up, Arsenal won the 2001 Premiership title with 87 points, setting a new club record. They also beat Chelsea 2–0 in the FA Cup Final, sealing the Club's third double. In 2003 Arsenal retained the FA Cup and then, in 2004, they won the Premiership, going through an entire League season without defeat. In 2006, the Club moved to a brand new home – Emirates Stadium.

THIERRY HENRY

TONY ADAMS

FRANK McLINTOCK

35

Emirates

First friendly match
Arsenal 2 Ajax 1
22 July 2006,
Dennis Bergkamp
Testimonial

There's a first time for everything and at the end of Arsenal's first season at its new home, there have been a flurry of first-time facts to report. So, who were the first Champions League opponents, who set up the first Arsenal goal and who scored the first goal against Spurs. Read on and find out...

First Arsenal goal at the North End
Gilberto v Aston Villa
19 August 2006

First referee
Graham Poll v Aston Villa

First disallowed goal
Kolo Toure v Aston Villa
(Offside)

First Arsenal goal
Gilberto v Aston Villa

First Arsenal assist
Theo Walcott
v Aston Villa

First competitive goal
Olof Mellberg
for Aston Villa,
19 August 2006

First international match
Brazil 3 Argentina 0
3 September 2006

First attendance
60,023 v Aston Villa

First Arsenal Premiership victory
Arsenal 3 Sheffield United 0
23 September 2006

First UEFA Champions League goal
Freddie Ljungberg v Dinamo Zagreb
23 August 2006

First UEFA Champions League match
Arsenal 2 Dinamo Zagreb 1
23 August 2006

First Arsenal goal at the South End
Thierry Henry v Porto, 26 September 2006

Firsts

First competitive line-up
Arsenal 1 Aston Villa 1,
19 August 2006 (Premiership)
1 Lehmann, 27 Eboue, 5 Toure, 20 Djourou,
31 Hoyte, 13 Hleb, 4 Fabregas, 19 Gilberto,
8 Ljungberg, 25 Adebayor, 14 Henry.
Subs: 11 van Persie (for Adebayor, 66)
32 Walcott (for Ljungberg, 73) 16 Flamini
(for Hoyte, 80), 24 Almunia, 18 Cygan.

First goalless game
Arsenal 0 CSKA Moscow 0
1 November 2006

First goal against Tottenham Hotspur
Emmanuel Adebayor

**First goal against
Manchester United**
Robin van Persie
21 January 2007

First FA Cup match
Arsenal 1 Bolton
Wanderers 1
28 January 2007

First Carling Cup match
Arsenal 3 Tottenham Hotspur 1
31 January 2007

First time Arsenal conceded more than one goal
Arsenal 2 Portsmouth 2, 16 December 2006

The first eight Premiership matches at Emirates
Stadium all ended either 3-0 or 1-1. The results are
listed for you below. So much for the old adage of
1-0 to the Arsenal!

Freaky Facts!

Arsenal 1 Aston Villa 1 - 19 August 2006
Arsenal 1 Middlesbrough 1 - 9 September 2006
Arsenal 3 Sheffield United 0 - 23 September 2006
Arsenal 3 Watford 0 - 14 October 2006
Arsenal 1 Everton 1 - 28 October 2006
Arsenal 3 Liverpool 0 - 12 November 2006
Arsenal 1 Newcastle United 1 - 18 November 2006
Arsenal 3 Tottenham Hotspur 0 - 2 December 2006

First hat-trick
Jay Simpson v Cardiff City
19 February 2007, FA Youth Cup

THE EUROSTARS!

On 7 June 2008, the European Championships will kick-off in Basle, Switzerland. Matches will be played in both Switzerland and Austria in the second European Championship tournament to be co-hosted – in 2000 Belgium and Holland were co-hosts. This will be the 13th European Championships and many Arsenal players took part in their respective countries' bid to qualify!

DENMARK

Nicklas Bendtner's goal against Germany in March 2007 brought to an end an eight-match unbeaten sequence for Joachim Low's men. Luckily, Jens Lehmann had been rested for the friendly so there were no hard feelings back at Arsenal! Since their unlikely tournament victory in 1992, the Danes have always been optimistic of further success!

ENGLAND

Destined for a long career at international level, Theo Walcott has already famously been part of the squad at a tournament – the 2006 World Cup! Due in part to his shoulder injury, he was only on the fringes of England's qualification campaign but he will hope for a place for England – and for him – in Switzerland and Austria.

FRANCE

Winners in 1984 and 2000, the French always fancy themselves to do well when it comes to the big tournaments. William Gallas (pictured) starred in the 2004 European Championships and was a rock for France in the 2008 qualification competition. Gael Clichy and Abou Diaby will also be looking to play influential roles for their country in Austria and Switzerland during the summer of 2008.

SPAIN

The Spaniards were winners in 1964. As they attempted to reach the 2008 finals, who better to marshall their midfield than Cesc Fabregas who was player of the tournament for the 2003 Fifa under-17 World Cup, and a key player in the 2004 Uefa under-17 European Championships?

38

SWEDEN

One of his country's most experienced internationals, Freddie Ljungberg will be celebrating his tenth year of service for the Swedes in 2008. He has already played in two European Championships and one World Cup.

HOLLAND

The Dutch were the champions of Europe in 1988 and are always keen to repeat that triumph. Due to injury, Robin van Persie did not play as big a part in the qualifications as he'd have liked but remains a key figure in the squad.

BELARUS

Having been a key player in his country's 2004 European Championship under-21 finals, Alexander Hleb is now a regular for the first team. His younger brother Slava is also an international for Belarus!

CZECH REPUBLIC

Winners, as Czechoslovakia back in 1976, and runners-up when the tournament was held in England in 1996, the Czech Republic remain a hugely respected force on the European scene. Tomas Rosicky made his international debut in 2000 and was a tireless figure as he aimed for his third successive European Championships finals.

GERMANY

Winners of the tournament in 1972, 1980 and 1996, the Germans had the safe hands of Jens Lehmann to guide them through the qualification matches. Fresh from a spectacular 2006 World Cup, Jens was a dependable presence.

SWITZERLAND

As co-hosts, the Swiss automatically qualified for the tournament. However, they kept themselves busy with a series of friendly matches in which the Arsenal defensive pair of Philippe Senderos and Johan Djourou featured.

39

GUNNERSAURUS
EMIRATES STADIUM TOUR

As Gunnersaurus can visit almost every part of Emirates Stadium, no one is better qualified to give you a guided tour of this great example of modern architecture.

Exterior Canons
"Welcome to Emirates Stadium! I will be your tour guide for the day. I hope you enjoy it!"

Directors' Box
"Make yourself comfortable in these comfy seats. This is where the Club's hardworking Directors sit to watch the match!"

Trophy Cabinet
"Ooh! Look at all that lovely silverware on display. Very impressive!

THE DEEPER
ME CAPSULE PLACED ON 28TH OCTOBER 2004

Time Capsule
"This capsule includes all manner of memorabilia including a piece of Highbury turf. Posh!"

Diamond Club
"Recognise this clock? It's a replica of the one that stood proudly above the Clock End at Highbury."

Players Entrance
"If you grow up to play for Arsenal, this will be where you'll hang out before each home game."

Changing Rooms
"A change is as good as a rest so come on in and see there the players get changed."

Changing Rooms
"Ooh, you could swing a cat in here. You could even swing a dinosaur but don't even go there!"

Showers
"The current Arsenal team is so great it is showered not just with water but with praise!"

Hydropool
"This is a special pool that helps keep the players in tip-top condition. A yellow card for any divers!"

Physio Room
"Ooh I'm feeling a bit stiff. Hopefully Gary Lewin the physio can help get me back into shape!"

Press Conference Room
"Feeling better already! Next question please?"

Tunnel
"I say, Mr Wenger, please can I have a game this afternoon?"

Groundsman's Office
"Ever wondered who keeps the pitch and Stadium looking so great? It's the Groundsman and this is where he sits. Excuse me while I check my emails."

Tractor Shed
"Ooo-aarr! I thought it was Ipswich Town who were known as the Tractor Boys!"

The Armoury
"No need to leave here empty-handed!"

41

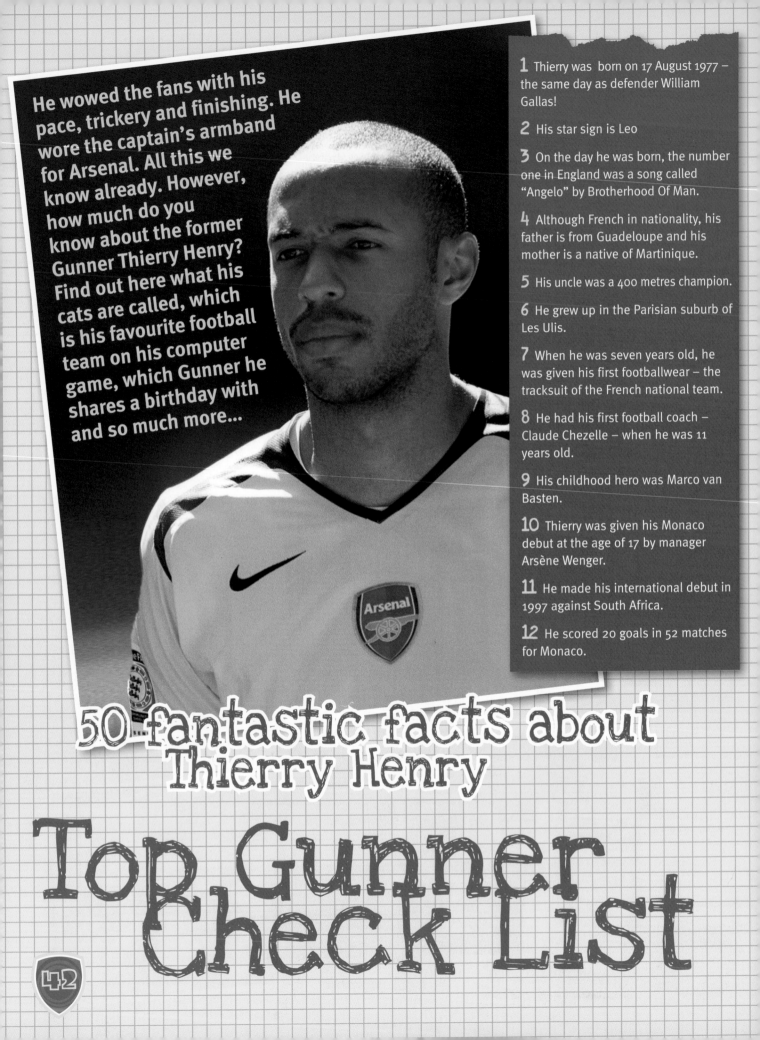

He wowed the fans with his pace, trickery and finishing. He wore the captain's armband for Arsenal. All this we know already. However, how much do you know about the former Gunner Thierry Henry? Find out here what his cats are called, which is his favourite football team on his computer game, which Gunner he shares a birthday with and so much more...

1 Thierry was born on 17 August 1977 – the same day as defender William Gallas!

2 His star sign is Leo

3 On the day he was born, the number one in England was a song called "Angelo" by Brotherhood Of Man.

4 Although French in nationality, his father is from Guadeloupe and his mother is a native of Martinique.

5 His uncle was a 400 metres champion.

6 He grew up in the Parisian suburb of Les Ulis.

7 When he was seven years old, he was given his first footballwear – the tracksuit of the French national team.

8 He had his first football coach – Claude Chezelle – when he was 11 years old.

9 His childhood hero was Marco van Basten.

10 Thierry was given his Monaco debut at the age of 17 by manager Arsène Wenger.

11 He made his international debut in 1997 against South Africa.

12 He scored 20 goals in 52 matches for Monaco.

50 fantastic facts about Thierry Henry

Top Gunner Check List

13 On 17 October 2005 he became Arsenal's top goalscorer of all time with two strikes against Sparta Prague.

14 He is married to Nicole Merry (pictured right).

15 He says his father is a perfectionist who helped him enormously when he was starting in football – "His influence is always with me, whether it's in the Premiership or the World Cup."

16 His nickname is 'Titi'.

17 He dreams of still playing for France in time for the 2010 World Cup – "I would love to play in the first World Cup in Africa."

18 In 2003 he finished runner-up to fellow Frenchman Zinedine Zidane in the Player of the Year poll.

19 His daughter is called Tea Henry.

20 He was named one of the 125 Greatest Living Footballers by Pele in March 2004.

21 He started a campaign to fight racism in football called "Stand Up, Speak Out".

22 He has appeared in television advertisements for Renault in which he made famous the term "va, va voom".

23 He is friends with NBA star Tony Parker.

24 He was the PFA Player Of The Year in 2003 and 2004.

25 In April 2004 he scored seven goals in two games: three against Liverpool and then four against Leeds United.

26 He is 6ft 2in tall.

27 In the 2002–03 season, he was responsible for a record-breaking 20 assists.

28 It took him 25 minutes to drive to the Arsenal training ground in the morning.

29 He eats his lunch late in the afternoon – "I know it's kind of a Spanish thing," he says.

30 He says he discussed "private stuff" with Arsène Wenger "probably once every two or three months".

31 When he plays Pro Evolution Soccer, he plays not as Arsenal but as Saudi Arabia.

32 He has two cats called Jungle and Cookie.

33 When he first arrived at Arsenal, he was presented with a video tape of all Ian Wright's goals for the Club Inspiration indeed!

34 He made his Arsenal debut against Leicester City on 7 August 1999.

35 As well as football, Thierry is also good at athletics, basketball and handball.

36 He wishes he had been present when tennis player Yannick Noah won the French Open in 1983.

37 His best friends in football are Patrick Vieira and David Trezeguet.

38 He scored 8 hat-tricks at Highbury.

39 He doesn't understand the rules of cricket.

40 He scored the winner in the 2003 Confederations Cup Final.

41 He jokes that if he could change one rule in football, it would be "that as long as my team is losing, the referee cannot end the game!"

42 He was France's top scorer in the 1998 World Cup finals and 2000 European Championship finals.

43 He is full of praise for former manager Arsène Wenger, even at his own expense – "To deal with me must be a pain!" he smiles.

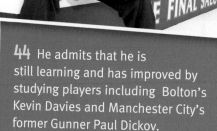

44 He admits that he is still learning and has improved by studying players including Bolton's Kevin Davies and Manchester City's former Gunner Paul Dickov.

45 He donated the £27,000 prize for winning the 2005–06 Golden Boot to Bob Wilson's Willow Foundation.

46 After he broke Ian Wright's all-time scoring record for Arsenal, one of the first phone calls of congratulation he received came from…Ian Wright.

47 He was the Football Writers' Player Of The Year for 2003, 2004 and 2006.

48 He was the most popular Premiership footballer in Kenya and Tanzania according to a poll conducted by the BBC.

49 He was Media Personality Of The Year in 2005, awarded by the Commission For Racial Equality.

50 He is an international brand ambassador for Tommy Hilfiger's formal and underwear ranges. Suits you, sir!

MIND YOUR LANGUAGE!

We love you Arsenal, we do.
Oh, Arsenal we love you!

On t'aime Arsenal, on t'aime.
Oh Arsenal qu'est ce qu'on t'aime!

Come on you Reds!
Allez les rouges!

One nil to the Arsenal!
Un zéro pour Arsenal!

You're not singing, you're not singing, you're not singing anymore!
Vous ne chantez plus, vous ne chantez plus, vous ne chantez plus, maintenant!

There's only one Gael Clichy!
Il y en a qu'un Gael Clichy!

We love you Arsenal, we do.
Oh, Arsenal we love you!

¡Te queremos Arsenal, oh sí!
¡Oh, querido Arsenal!

Come on you Reds!
¡Adelante los Rojos!

One nil to the Arsenal!
¡Uno a cero al Arsenal!

You're not singing, you're not singing, you're not singing anymore!
¡Ya no cantáis, ya no cantáis, ya no cantáis más!

There's only one Cesc Fabregas!
¡Sólo hay un Cesc Fabregas!

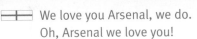

FRENCH

SPANISH

Without the songs and chants that ring out from the stands, watching football would not be half as much fun. In common with all Premiership teams, Arsenal now have a truly international squad. Should you ever take a trip on the Arsenal team-bus, this football phrasebook will help you communicate with the players in their own tongues ...

We love you Arsenal, we do. Oh, Arsenal we love you!
Wij houden van Arsenal, voor altijd. Arsenal, wij houden van jou!

Come on you Reds!
Kom maar op, jullie rooien!

One nil to the Arsenal!
Één–nul voor Arsenal!

You're not singing, you're not singing, you're not singing anymore!
Jullie zingen niet, jullie zingen niet, jullie zingen nooit meer!

There's only one Robin van Persie!
Er is maar een Robin van Persie!

We love you Arsenal, we do. Oh, Arsenal we love you!
Wir lieben Euch, Arsenal. Oh Arsenal, wir lieben Euch!

Come on you Reds!
Los die Roten!

One nil to the Arsenal!
Eins zu null für die Arsenal!

You're not singing, you're not singing, you're not singing anymore!
Ihr singt nicht mehr, Ihr singt nicht mehr, Ihr singt überhaupt nicht mehr!

There's only one Jens Lehmann!
Es gibt nur einen Jens Lehmann!

DUTCH

GERMAN

45

STAT ATTACK!

The 2006–07 season was full of drama and excitement as Arsenal Football Club settled in at Emirates Stadium. Both home and away, the Gunners played some fantastic football and got some great results. Here are all the stats and facts you need to know about a memorable campaign...

LEAGUE TABLE

	P	W	D	L	F	A	GD	Pts
1 Manchester United	38	28	5	5	83	27	56	89
2 Chelsea	38	24	11	3	64	24	40	83
3 Liverpool	38	20	8	10	57	27	30	68
4 Arsenal	38	19	11	8	63	35	28	68

GREAT GOAL

Thierry Henry v Blackburn Rovers – 13 January 2007
Thierry raced down the left wing with the ball at his feet. The Frenchman then played a one-two with Cesc Fabregas and received the ball 20 yards from goal, slightly to the left of centre. Brad Friedel could only get a fingertip to Henry's wonderfully fierce and accurate shot.

Most minutes played in the Premiership (max 3,420)

Jens Lehmann – 3,261
Cesc Fabregas – 3,204
Kolo Toure – 3,171
Gilberto – 2,955
Alexander Hleb – 2,370

Top goalscorers (all competitions)

Robin van Persie – 13
Thierry Henry – 12
Emmanuel Adebayor – 12
Gilberto – 11
Julio Baptista – 10

Most appearances (all competitions)

Kolo Toure – 53
Cesc Fabregas – 49 (+5 sub)
Gilberto – 46 (+1 sub)
Jens Lehmann – 44
Alexander Hleb – 40 (+8 sub)

STAR MAN

GILBERTO

In the absence of Thierry Henry, Gilberto captained Arsenal – and what an example he was! Protecting the back four, winning tackles and distributing the ball with accuracy, the Brazilian was in awesome form. He wasn't exactly shy in front of goal, either – he scored 11 times including penalties against Tottenham Hotspur and Fulham.

CLASSIC MATCH

PREMIERSHIP

Arsenal 2, Manchester United 1 – 21 January 2007

In a season packed with games featuring late drama, this match stood out for particular last-gasp excitement. Wayne Rooney's goal after 53 minutes was cancelled out after 83 minutes by Robin van Persie. Then, deep into injury time, Henry headed the winner to confirm a league double over United and send Emirates Stadium into raptures of joy.

CLASSIC MATCH

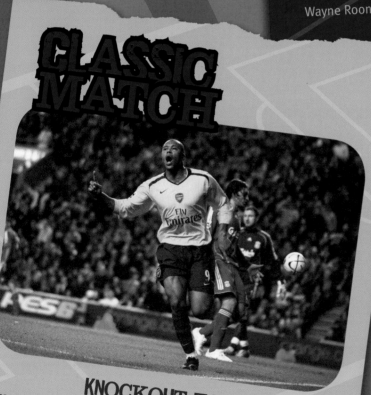

KNOCKOUT TOURNAMENTS

Liverpool 3, Arsenal 6 – January 9, 2007

Julio Baptista arrived at Anfield without a goal in English football to his name and left a few hours later with the match-ball under his arm after an extraordinary four-goal performance. Full of excitement, this victory set up a semi-final tie against Tottenham Hotspur.

Biggest wins

Carling Cup
Liverpool 3 Arsenal 6 – 9 January 2007
FA Cup
Liverpool 1 Arsenal 3 – 6 January 2007
Bolton Wanderers 1 Arsenal 3 – 14 February 2007
UEFA Champions League
Arsenal 3 Dynamo Zagreb 0 – 8 August 2006
Premiership
Arsenal 6 Blackburn Rovers 2 – 23 December 2006

Highest Attendance

60,132
Premiership
Arsenal 2, Reading 1
3 March 2007

47

Which three sports would always make you turn off the television?

Golf, cricket and darts. (Thierry Henry)

Which one item would you like with you if you were marooned on a desert island?

A phone – with some credit on it! (Emmanuel Eboue)

What is your favourite tourist attraction in London?

The National Gallery. (Mathieu Flamini)

RANDOM

Down the years, the folks at The Official Arsenal Magazine have grilled many first-teamers – and occasionally members of the coaching staff – about their likes and dislikes. These quizzes have prompted all sorts of random, entertaining and sometimes amusing responses from members of the team. So if you've ever lain awake at night wondering which Gunner likes salmon on his pizza, what Philippe Senderos makes of the London Underground or whether Mathieu Flamini understands the rules to curling, then read our selection of answers received to the quick, quirky questions...

RAPID

What is the craziest rumour you've read about yourself?

That I could run the 100 metres in under 11 seconds when I was 10 years old! A bit crazy. (Theo Walcott)

What is your favourite pizza topping?

Bolognese. (Alexandre Song)

What do you remember about your first day at Arsenal?

I remember smiling. That was all I did on my first day here. (Gael Clichy)

What would you be doing if you weren't a footballer?

Maybe a photojournalist. (Alexander Hleb)

What was the first kit you owned?

It was a Brazil kit which I wore all the time when I was about seven or eight. It was a big shirt with a small number ten on the back so it looked quite funny. I thought I was Romario! (Johan Djourou)

Do you ever use the London Underground?

Yes, quite a lot. I think it's really good and easy to use but it's strange how nobody ever speaks to each other! (Philippe Senderos)

Name three other sports you are good at.

Table-tennis, tennis and pool. (Robin van Persie)

Do you prefer shopping or sleeping?

Sleeping. (Alexander Hleb)

RESPONSES

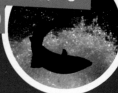

What is your favourite pizza topping?

Salmon. (Denilson)

What is your favourite chart music?

That's a difficult question to answer. I would have to say I like all music. (Abou Diaby)

What would you be doing if you weren't a footballer?

I've no idea because I've been playing football from the age of seven! (Jeremie Aliadiere)

Is there any sport you do not understand the rules to?

Curling. It is very strange. (Mathieu Flamini)

EMMANUEL ADEBAYOR

Gianlugi Buffon

A very good goalkeeper, very quick and sharp with valuable World Cup experience.

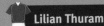
Lilian Thuram

One of the best players in this team – a real gem. He's the person who would talk to his defence and keep everyone together.

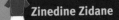
Kolo Toure

Another sharp and strong player with tons of experience. An invaluable footballer for this team.

Tony Adams

He was excellent at defending and I think he would do a great job in this fantasy team.

Roberto Carlos

Another experienced player and somebody who knows the right balance between attack and defence.

Zinedine Zidane

Zizou is a magical player who can change a game in an instant.

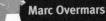
Deco

He is a player with great skills, can score from anywhere and is a great passer of the ball.

Marc Overmars

Technically gifted and exceptionally fast. He'd provide the service for my strikers.

Pele

Another legend of the game, every young footballer wants to be like him.

Nwankwo Kanu

Kanu is my hero and a great, great player.

Diego Maradona

He's the man! Magic.

ELEMENTARY MY DEAR ARSENAL

Abou Diaby was nicknamed "Le Nettoyer" by Thierry Henry – it means "the cleaner" in French!

ABOU DIABY

Gianlugi Buffon

He's simply the best; you would want him in your team.

Gianluca Zambrotta

He had a fantastic 2006 World Cup and is definitely one of the best in his position.

Fabio Cannavaro

He may be small but he is very powerful and would form a brilliant partnership with Lilian.

Lilian Thuram

I've always liked him and the two centre-backs in this team work really well together.

Ashley Cole

There are a few left-backs to choose from but I don't see past Ashley as first choice. He's one of the best in the world.

Zinedine Zidane

The best, despite his 'argument' with Materazzi.

Patrick Vieira

An excellent player and one who would work well in this team.

Claude Makelele

With him and Patrick Vieira in midfield it would be like a wall in front of the defence.

Ronaldinho

You'd just have to put him in a team like this!

Thierry Henry

Who else? He's proven that he is one of the best and will continue to be so for some time.

Ronaldo

A lot has been said of him and his weight, but to me he is still one of the best strikers to have played football.

Arsenal players are heroes to every Gunners fan but who are their footballing idols? Find out here with the 'Dream Teams' of Emmanuel Adebayor, Abou Diaby, Cesc Fabregas and Theo Walcott.

CESC FABREGAS

Iker Casillas

He's still very young but he dominates his goal. He's very solid.

Lilian Thuram

A very good player who keeps running for the whole 90 minutes. Equally good as a defender and when going forward.

Sol Campbell

His presence on the pitch makes all the forwards on the opposition respect him. It was great to play alongside him.

Kolo Toure

Like Sol, incredibly strong and makes great runs forward. He is good with the ball and can also set up and score goals himself.

Roberto Carlos

He is a very good defender and excellent going forward. I saw how good he was when I played against Brazil for the Catalonia team in 2004.

Zinedine Zidane

Pure quality. His passing was always excellent and the ball always went where he wanted it to go. He was consistent, too.

Patrick Vieira

Always manages to win the ball. Makes a lot of runs, both with and without the ball. Leads by example and is great to learn from.

Josep Guardiola

I used to really enjoy watching him when he was at his best. I was with him when he was at Barcelona and I always looked up to him.

Ronaldinho

He can take on and beat defenders, and can play anywhere on the pitch. He's great to watch and is another one who I have played against.

Thierry Henry

I think he's the best in the world. He is so strong and is capable of changing a game or winning it on his own.

Ronaldo

With Thierry, he's one of the best in the world. Very strong, he scores goals in whatever team he is playing.

THEO WALCOTT

Gianlugi Buffon

He once came second in the European Player of the Year award which is a great achievement for a goalkeeper.

Lilian Thuram

A good strong quick athletic defender, he is everything you want from a right-back.

John Terry

I've trained with him for England and he's just so difficult to get past. He's a great presence in the defence.

Fabio Cannavaro

He was named European Footballer of the Year for 2006, which tells you everything. He had a fantastic World Cup for Italy.

Ashley Cole

Another player I've trained with and, again, very hard to beat one-on-one. He has great pace, too.

Cristiano Ronaldo

For me he's one of the best wingers about at the moment; good on the ball, with plenty of skills.

Kaka

I really like the way he gets forward to support the attack. He gets plenty of goals from midfield too.

Steven Gerrard

I've chosen him for his goals from midfield, and his excellent work-rate. A great all-rounder.

Ronaldinho

A fantastic player, did you see the overhead goal he scored against Villarreal? A World Player of the Year.

Thierry Henry

My idol. It was fantastic to train with him, to see how good he is every day. I've learnt so much from him.

Samuel Eto'o

I like his movement, running off the ball and excellent finishing. I think he's a similar type of player to Thierry.

GUNNERSAURUS'
A-Z of Arsenal!

A is for August - the month of my birth in 1993.

HI, I'M GUNNERSAURUS, THE CLUB MASCOT. HAVE YOU EVER WANTED TO KNOW MORE ABOUT MY LIFE, MY VIEWS AND OTHER SECRET DINOSAUR DELIGHTS? I THOUGHT YOU MIGHT, SO HERE IS MY A-Z OF ARSENAL THAT SHOULD TELL YOU EVERYTHING YOU EVER WANTED TO KNOW ABOUT ME. AND POSSIBLY A BIT MORE BESIDES!

B is for Bergkamp - I still miss ya, Dennis!

C is for Champions, which Arsenal have been 13 times!

52

D is for Dynamo Kiev - I travelled all the way to the Ukraine for an away match once - visiting the Children's Centre in Chernigov while I was about it.

E is for Emirates Stadium - the finest football ground on the planet!

F is for Fred the Red - I once scored a penalty against the Manchester United mascot. Not that I like to go on about it.

G is for Goals - easily the best part of any match and, thanks to Robin and the lads, there are always plenty around when Arsenal take the field!

I is for Ideal - Arsenal is an ideal club, after all!

H is for How Do They Do That? - when the super-skilled Gunners play some of the finest football known to man, it's hard to work out how they pull off their tricks!

J is for Junior Gunners - where the coolest kids hang out and the most dashing dinosaur.

K is for kickabout - nothing like getting a load of mates together and playing some football, is there?

L is for Lehmann - daring blocks, penalty stops and entertainment galore: here's to ya, Jens!

M is for the Millennium Stadium - Bah! Been there, done that. Arsenal reached so many finals in Cardiff that it became virtually my second home for a while.

N is for the Natural History Museum - I went there with 50 Junior Gunners once. There were so many of my ancestors there, it was like Jurassic Park!

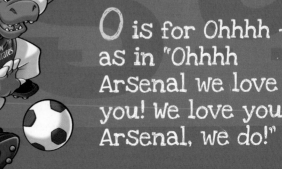

O is for Ohhhh - as in "Ohhhh Arsenal we love you! We love you Arsenal, we do!"

P is for Pre-Match Entertainment - I always love hanging out on the pitch before a big game, soaking up the atmosphere.

Q is for quality - the word that sums up the Club from top to bottom

S is for Strikers - Robin, Theo, Emmanuel, Nicklas - we're not short of ace attackers!

R is for Rex - This is my surname. But you don't have to call me "Mr Rex". Just "Sir" will do fine!

T is for Tottenham Hotspur - I know, boo! But a "hurrah" for me, I once scored a penalty against Chirpy, the Spurs mascot.

U is for Unbelievable! - Ever found yourself shouting that word after another Arsenal masterclass?

V is for Victory - Nothing like one, is there?

W is for Wenger - Hats off to the French genius!

X is for X Factor - Something you need to have to join Arsenal.

Y is for Yippee! - it's what I shout when Arsenal score!

Z is for Zzzzzzzzzzz - I always sleep well at night and enjoy sweet dreams about life at the greatest Football Club in the world.

TRIVIA QUIZ

ON THE DEFENSIVE

1. The average age of the Arsenal back four that played at Stamford Bridge was: 21, 31 or 25?
2. Lauren and Sol Campbell both left Arsenal for which south coast side?
3. William Gallas and which other defender scored in the 3–0 home Premiership win over Liverpool?
4. What nationality is left-back Gael Clichy?
5. Which side did William Gallas join Arsenal from?
6. Armand Traore was born in which city?
7. What number shirt did Philippe Senderos and Arsenal legend Tony Adams both wear?
8. What nationality is Justin Hoyte?
9. Which national side does Emmanuel Eboue play for?
10. What number did William Gallas inherit from Dennis Bergkamp?

Are You An Arsenal Know-All?

Have you been keeping your eyes and ears open?

Are you Arsenal's most knowledgeable fan? Then prove it by answering our quiz. With five sections of 10 questions each, this is a marathon not a sprint. Will you finish in the lead?

IT'S A KNOCKOUT!

11. Who were Arsenal's first opponents in the 2006–07 Carling Cup?
12. And who did the Gunners face first in the 2006–07 FA Cup?
13. Who scored the winner against Everton in the Carling Cup?
14. True or false: Arsenal played no home ties in the Carling Cup campaign.
15. How many goals were scored in total when Arsenal played Liverpool in the Carling Cup?
16. In which month did Arsenal play their first Carling Cup match of 2006–07?
17. Mart Poom made his Arsenal debut in a Carling Cup tie. Who were the opponents?
18. Who scored twice as Arsenal beat Liverpool 3–1 in the FA Cup?
19. And who scored the Gunners' other goal in the same tie?
20. Who scored an own goal and then two at the other end in one Carling Cup tie against Tottenham Hotspur?

MIDDLE OF THE PACK

21. What nationality is Cesc Fabregas?
22. Which Arsenal midfielder is a World Cup winner?
23. Which midfielder scored the winner in Arsenal's first ever win at Emirates Stadium?
24. True or false: Freddie Ljungberg has never captained Arsenal.
25. What nationality is Alexander Hleb?
26. Tomas Rosicky comes from which country?
27. Abou Diaby joined Arsenal from which club?
28. Denilson made his Arsenal debut in which competition?
29. What nationality is Freddie Ljungberg?
30. Which team did Mathieu Flamini play for before he joined Arsenal?

HISTORY LESSON

31 In 1994, Arsenal beat Parma to win which European trophy?

32 Which Yorkshire team did former Arsenal boss George Graham manage?

33 Who captained Arsenal to Football League and Premiership titles in 1989, 1991, 1998 and 2002?

34 From which club did Dennis Bergkamp join Arsenal?

35 Arsenal won the FA Cup and League Cup in 1993. Which team were the opponents in both finals?

36 Arsenal beat which team to win the 1979 FA Cup Final?

37 Who did Ian Wright play for before he joined Arsenal?

38 True or false: Arsenal won the double in 1998.

39 Who scored the Gunners' famous title-clinching winner at Anfield in May 1989?

40 Against which club did Arsenal play their final match at Highbury?

STRIKE A LIGHT!

41 Who was the first striker to score in the Premiership for Arsenal during the 2006–07 season?

42 Against which team was this goal scored?

43 With which League club did Theo Walcott start his career?

44 What nationality is Robin van Persie?

45 Against which side did Emmanuel Adebayor score his first goal of the 2006–07 Premiership campaign?

46 In which country was Jeremie Aliadiere born?

47 Theo Walcott scored twice for the England Under-21s against which country in October 2006?

48 True or false: Emmanuel Adebayor has won 17 caps for France.

49 To which club did Jose Antonio Reyes move on loan?

50 Which Arsenal striker wore the 25 shirt, now Emmanuel Adebayor's number, for five seasons until 2004?

PICTURE QUIZ

Find the well-known word, name or phrase made by these pictures or groups of pictures. They are all linked by the theme of Arsenal Football Club.

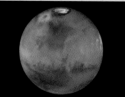

MENTHOL·COUGH SUPPRESSANT 9 DROPS

Bureau de Change

XWORD

ACROSS

1. Dutch team who played Arsenal in 2006–07 Champions League (9)
7. Spanish giants who signed Jose Antonio Reyes on loan (4)
8. What you'd use to buy a programme (4)
9. The Dennis Bergkamp _ _ _ at Arsenal was from 1995 to 2006 (3)
12. An angry ball played into the penalty area from the wing (5)
13. Muscle spasm caused by tiredness (5)
16. Number worn by William Gallas (3)
18. Common abbreviation of Mr Hleb's first name (4)
19. Gilberto was _ _ _ _ on 17 October 1976 (4)
20. Club against which Julio Baptista scored four times in the Carling Cup (9)

DOWN

2. Former Arsenal man Luis Boa Morte was an unused sub for Portugal in their 2006 World Cup match against this Middle East country (4)
3. Arsenal's club captain in 2006–07 (5)
4. A stern test (4)
5. Arsène Wenger is one of these, so is Robert Pires (9)
6. What Arsenal were in 2004 (9)
10. Country against which Tomas Rosicky scored twice in the 2006 World Cup finals (1,1,1)
11. If you control the ball with this it's still handball (3)
14. How often Arsenal have been relegated since 1919 (5)
15. _ _ _ _-final, the stage where Arsenal's kids beat Spurs in the Carling Cup (4)
17. Top defender, Mr Toure (4)

In 2006–07, Arsenal played at 26 different grounds in the Premiership, FA Cup, Carling Cup and UEFA Champions League. They have all been cunningly hidden in this word search, written in a straight line, either up or down, across or backwards, even diagonally. No letters have been missed out. In case you can't remember where the 26 are, this is the list:

E	M	I	R	A	T	E	S	A	N	A	S	I	R	O	O	D	T	R	A	F
A	N	F	E	L	D	W	H	I	T	E	H	A	R	T	L	A	N	E	T	R
S	G	N	B	J	J	O	N	A	T	O	D	E	R	D	D	O	A	E	R	A
T	H	E	E	A	R	O	A	D	S	O	N	P	A	R	T	I	R	E	N	T
L	D	D	C	M	W	D	S	T	R	E	E	P	A	R	R	K	T	B	E	T
A	O	N	C	A	E	P	G	B	A	O	R	A	D	R	A	G	A	O	D	O
N	D	E	A	K	R	A	F	R	E	R	X	E	D	E	F	S	T	K	I	N
D	E	H	W	S	D	R	D	A	D	D	D	D	R	O	F	F	A	R	S	P
S	K	D	E	I	D	K	R	M	A	N	E	R	A	L	O	A	D	O	R	A
O	R	E	D	M	D	S	T	A	M	F	O	R	D	B	R	I	D	G	E	R
U	A	R	I	I	P	G	M	L	N	I	Z	Y	M	U	D	V	I	P	V	K
T	P	A	D	R	H	I	L	L	D	F	Q	D	E	A	I	U	M	P	I	J
H	S	T	D	S	I	S	L	L	A	A	I	U	U	L	D	S	U	I	R	T
A	E	E	O	L	L	E	L	A	E	Y	S	E	L	K	L	E	R	A	P	N
M	M	U	D	N	I	J	S	N	R	O	A	A	L	D	S	A	J	N	A	I
P	A	N	D	I	P	A	D	E	D	D	P	D	I	D	I	O	V	S	D	A
T	J	E	V	E	S	A	R	D	H	A	W	T	H	O	R	N	S	E	K	S
M	T	V	I	D	A	O	R	A	R	C	L	A	M	O	N	T	R	D	H	I
A	S	A	D	D	E	R	A	K	R	A	P	N	O	S	I	D	O	O	G	T
D	A	O	R	E	G	A	R	A	C	I	V	I	T	O	M	O	K	O	L	U
S	F	I	E	L	D	S	A	C	R	A	V	E	N	C	O	T	T	A	G	E

- [ ] EMIRATES
- [ ] VILLA PARK
- [ ] EWOOD PARK
- [ ] GOODISON PARK
- [ ] CRAVEN COTTAGE
- [ ] ANFIELD
- [ ] EASTLANDS
- [ ] OLD TRAFFORD
- [ ] REEBOK
- [ ] THE VALLEY
- [ ] STAMFORD BRIDGE
- [ ] RIVERSIDE
- [ ] ST JAMES PARK
- [ ] FRATTON PARK
- [ ] MADEJSKI
- [ ] BRAMALL LANE
- [ ] WHITE HART LANE
- [ ] VICARAGE ROAD
- [ ] UPTON PARK
- [ ] JJB
- [ ] MAKSIMIR
- [ ] DRAGAO
- [ ] AOL ARENA
- [ ] LOKOMOTIV
- [ ] PHILIPS
- [ ] HAWTHORNS

PUZZLES

SUDOKU

Place a number from 1 to 9 in each empty cell so that each row, each column and each 3 x 3 block contains all the numbers from 1 to 9.

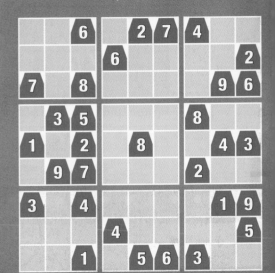

SPOT THE BALL

Where do you think the ball is?
– A, B, C, or D

SPOT THE DIFFERENCE

Can you spot the ten differences between the two photographs?

59

ANSWERS

PICTURE QUIZ

1. Robin Van Persie.
2. Gunners.
3. Marc Overmars.
4. Highbury.
5. Marble halls.
6. Emirates.

XWORD

ACROSS

1. Eindhoven
7. Real
8. Cash
9. Era
12. Cross
13. Cramp
16. Ten
18. Alex
19. Born
20. Liverpool

DOWN

2. Iran
3. Henry
4. Exam
5. Frenchman
6. Champions
10. USA
11. Arm
14. Never
15. Semi
17. Kolo

TRIVIA QUIZ

1. 21.
2. Portsmouth.
3. Kolo Toure.
4. French.
5. Chelsea.
6. Paris.
7. Six.
8. English.
9. Ivory Coast.
10. Ten.
11. West Bromwich Albion.
12. Liverpool.
13. Emmanuel Adebayor.
14. False; they were at home in the second leg of the semi-final against Spurs.
15. Nine.
16. October.
17. Everton.
18. Tomas Rosicky.
19. Thierry Henry.
20. Julio Baptista.
21. Spanish.
22. Gilberto.
23. Mathieu Flamini.
24. False.
25. Belarusian.
26. Czech Republic.
27. Auxerre.
28. Carling Cup against West Bromwich Albion.
29. Swedish.
30. Marseille.
31. European Cup Winners' Cup.
32. Leeds United.
33. Tony Adams.
34. Inter Milan.
35. Sheffield Wednesday.
36. Manchester United.
37. Crystal Palace.
38. True – it was in 1998.
39. Michael Thomas.
40. Wigan Athletic.
41. Thierry Henry.
42. Middlesbrough.
43. Southampton.
44. Dutch.
45. Manchester United.
46. France.
47. Germany.
48. False – he plays for Togo.
49. Real Madrid.
50. Nwankwo Kanu.

Wordsearch

```
E M I R A T E S A N A S I R O O D T R A F
A N F E L D W H I T E H A R T L A N E T R
S G N B J J O N A T O D E R D D O A E R A
T H E E A R O A D S O N P A R T I R E N T
L D C M W D S T R E E P A R R K T B E T T
A O N C A E P G B A O R A D R A G A O D O
N D E A K R A F R X E D E F S T K I N N
D E H W S D K R D D R O F F A R S A
S K D E I D K R M A N E R L O A O A D R A
O R E D M D S T A M F O R D B R I D G E R
U A R I P G M L N I Z Y M U D P V K J
T P A D R H I L L D F Q D E A I U M P J
H S T D S I S L L A A I U U L D S U I R
A E E O L L E L A E Y S E L K L E R A P N
M M U D N I J S N R O A A L D S A J N A I
P A N D I P A D E D D P D I D I O V S D A
T J E V E S A R D H A W T H O R N S E K S
M T V I D A O R A R C L A M O N T R D H I
A S A D D E R A K R A P N O S I D O O G T
D A O R A G A R A C I V I T O M O K O L U
S F I E L D S A C R A V E N C O T T A G E
```

SUDOKU

9	1	6	5	2	7	4	3	8
5	4	3	6	9	8	1	7	2
7	2	8	1	4	3	5	9	6
4	3	5	2	1	9	8	6	7
1	6	2	7	8	5	9	4	3
8	9	7	3	6	4	2	5	1
3	5	4	8	7	2	6	1	9
6	8	9	4	3	1	7	2	5
2	7	1	9	5	6	3	8	4

SPOT THE BALL

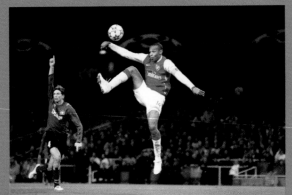

SPOT THE DIFFERENCE

WHERE'S GUNNERSAURUS?

60

WIN A FOOTBALL SIGNED BY YOUR ARSENAL HEROES!

The Arsenal players certainly know how to pass a football around the field. Well, how would you like to get your hands on a football that they've passed around the dressing-room so that each of them can sign it? That's right, we're offering you the chance to own a football signed by the Arsenal team. To stand a chance of winning this fantastic prize, simply answer the quiz below.
Good luck!

Q: Can you match the names of the following Arsenal players to their birthplace?

Cesc Fabregas	Rotterdam
Kolo Toure	Casal de Curacion
Robin van Persie	Sokuora Bouake
Alexander Hleb	Stanmore
Denilson	Minsk
Theo Walcott	Sao Paulo

WHERE'S GUNNERSAURUS?